To the loving memory of Snowball I:
You may be gone, but the mice
still fear for their lives.

HarperCollins books may be purchased for educational, business,
or sales promotional use. For information, please write:
Special Markets Department, HarperCollins Publishers, Inc.
10 East 53rd Street, New York, NY 10022

FIRST EDITION

ISBN 0-06-095212-1

96 97 98 99 00 RRD 10 9 8 7 6 5 4 3 2 1

Publisher: MATT GROENING
Managing Editor: JASON GRODE
Art Director / Editor: BILL MORRISON
Book Design: MARILYN FRANDSEN
Legal Guardian: SUSAN GRODE

Contributing Artists:
PETER ALEXANDER, TIM BAVINGTON, SHARON BRIDGEMAN,
SHAUN CASHMAN, JEANNINE CROWELL, STEPHANIE GLADDEN,
TIM HARKINS, NATHAN KANE, BILL MORRISON,
DAVID MOWRY, PHIL ORTIZ, CHRIS ROMAN, CHRIS UNGAR

Contributing Writers:
ADAM FEIN, TERRY DELEGEANE, SCOTT M. GIMPLE, GARY GLASBERG,
ANDREW GOTTLIEB, CLAY GRIFFITH, BILL MORRISON, JEFF ROSENTHAL,
SCOTT SHAW!, MARY TRAINOR, LONA WILLIAMS

PRINTED IN CANADA

CONTENTS

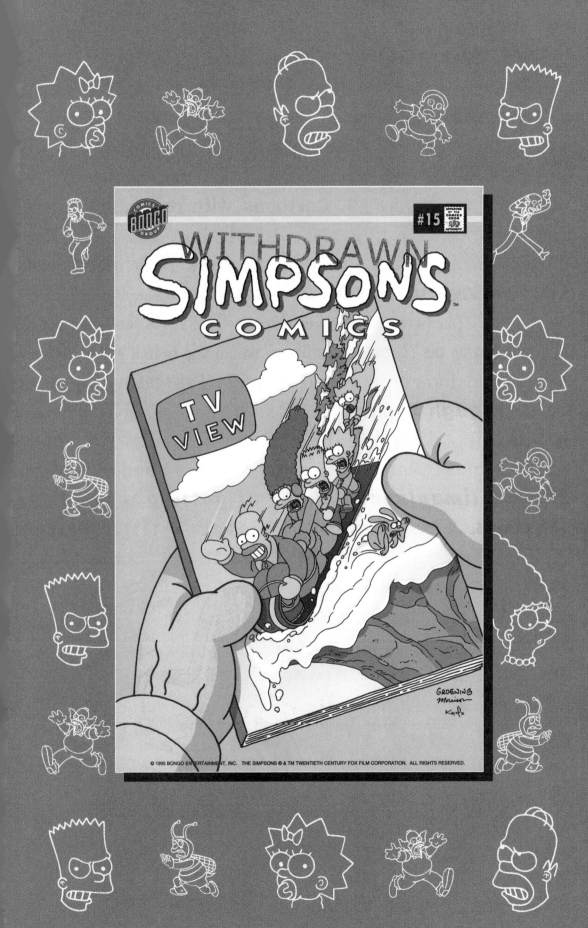

LISA'S TOP FORTY: 1. My baritone saxophone. 2. *The Happy Little Elves as a group.* **3. The Happy Little Elves individually: a. Yendor. b. Bubbles. c. Doofy. d. Moldy.** 4. The joy of overachievement. **5. Finding a surprise dessert in my lunchbox.** 6. Bleeding Gums Murphy. 7. Tetherball. *8. Seeing Bart get caught red-handed.* **9. Cartoons with redeeming social messages.** 10. *Looking on the bright side.* 11. Be-bop. 12. Playing both sides against the middle. **13. My friend Janey. 14. Corn-on-the-cob. 15. Television.** 16. *The way my baby sister smells right after her bath.* 17. The pursuit of happiness. 18. *Recess.* **19. The time I got all 50 states playing the "License Plate Game" on our trip to Hell Valley National Park.** 20. Any form of revenge on Bart. **21. Expressing my inner howl through music.** 22. Mom's cooking. **23. Moral superiority as a lifestyle.** 24. *Amelia Earhart.* **25. Those sprinkle things that go on top of ice cream and cupcakes.** *26. The (imagined) delight of getting a pony for Christmas.* 27. Snowball II. **28. Santa's Little Helper.** 29. Freedom of choice. *30. A Super-Deluxe Krusty Burger with bacon, chili, cheese and extra Krusty Secret Sauce.* **31. Ms. Hoover...on a good day. 32. Mr. Bergstrom any time.** 33. My dad's laugh. *34. Peace.* 35. The painful beauty of Emily Dickinson's verse. **36. Being a misunderstood creative genius.** 37. Daffodils. **38. Angst.** 39. Putting on a brave front. *40. And, in spite of everything, my family.*

HEY, MAN! WHAT HAPPENED TO THE ELECTRICITY?

≷FOOP≷

AAAA-AAAAH!

NO TV!!! CHRISTMAS IS RUINED!

AH, WHAT ARE YOU ALL BELLY-ACHING ABOUT? WHY, NERTZ, BACK IN MY DAY WE DIDN'T EVEN HAVE TV!

≷GASP!≷

OH MY GOSH!

THAT'S RIGHT! OL' SATAN HADN'T GOT AROUND TO IN-VENTING IT YET!

IMAGINE THAT! CHRISTMAS WITHOUT TELEVISION!

OOOOOOOOHHHHHHH!

:SHUDDER:

SO TELL US, GRAMPA, WHAT WAS IT LIKE BACK THEN?

YEAH, GRAMPA.... TELL US ABOUT WHEN *YOU* WERE A KID!

YES, GRAMPA. I THINK THE CHILDREN SHOULD HEAR HOW LIFE WAS *BEFORE* TELEVISION.

BEFORE TV STOLE OUR SOULS AWAY FROM US, YOU MEAN! *DEVILVISION*, I CALL IT! EXCEPT FOR MATLOCK, OF COURSE. MARK MY WORDS, WE'LL HAVE *BEELZEBUB* TO PAY FOR THIS...

YEAH, YEAH, GRAMPS... WE'RE ALL GONNA BURN IN HELL FOR WATCHING *TOP COPS!* WE GET THE PICTURE. NOW TELL US ABOUT WHEN YOU WERE A KID.

WELL, ALRIGHT THEN...

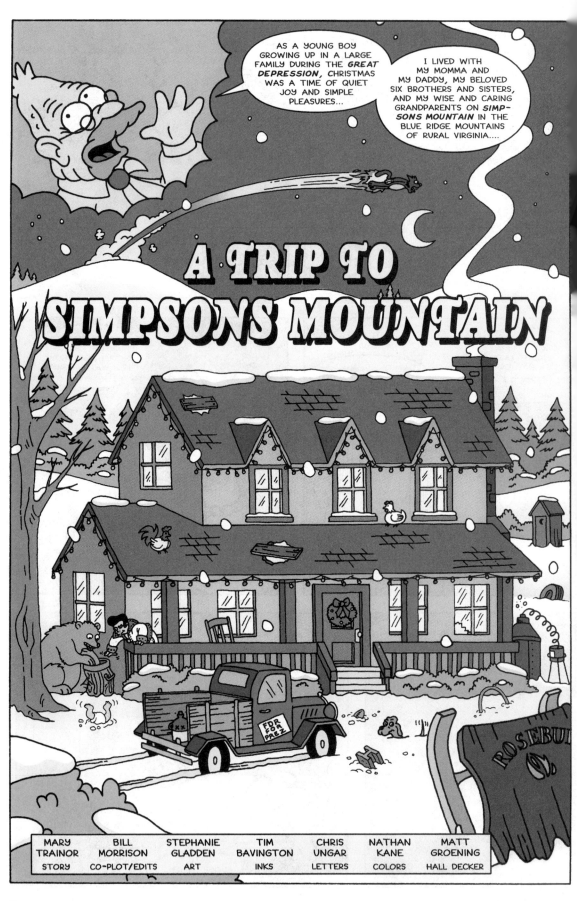

OUR FAMILY'S MODEST INCOME CAME FROM A *SAW MILL* THAT MY DADDY RAN WITH *GRAMPA ZEKE*...

LOOK OUT, YOU DERN *FOOL!* YOU'RE GONNA CUT OFF YOUR...

D'OH!!!

OURS WAS A LARGE BUT CLOSE-KNIT AND LOVING FAMILY...

LANDSAKES! I WISH THEY'D INVENT SOMETHING TO KEEP KIDS SITTING IN ONE PLACE...MAYBE SOME KIND OF *BOX* THAT *LIGHTS UP,* YOU KNOW... AND MAKES *SOUNDS...*

MOMMA, YOU'RE BABBLING. ARE YOU HAVING ONE OF YOUR *SPELLS?* YOU WANT ME TO FETCH YOUR *RE-LAXING MEDICINE?*

XXX

AND SO, I SET OFF TO FIND MY DADDY. I PASSED THE HOME OF THE ECCENTRIC *BALDWIN SISTERS*...

TRUDGE TRUDGE TRUDGE TRUDGE

LOOK, IT'S THAT WHITE TRASH *ABE-BOY SIMPSON*. EVERY *CHRISTMAS EVE* HIS DADDY GOES OFF ON A BENDER AND *OLIDIA* SENDS THAT FOOL KID OUT LOOKING FOR HIM.

GOODNESS GRACIOUS. PEOPLE LIKE THAT GIVE *DRINKING* A BAD NAME.

YES, SISTER. THAT'S WHY WE MUST TAKE CARE TO SHARE OUR "RECIPE" WITH ONLY THE FINER FOLKS IN THIS TOWN...

...THE ONES WITH THE CHARM AND BREEDING TO BE ALCOHOLICS...NOT MERE DRUNKARDS!

OH, AND LOOK, SISTER. HERE COMES OUR OWN *REVEREND REED!*

LET'S GET OUT THE GOOD CRYSTAL 8-OUNCE TUMBLERS, SHALL WE?

DURING *THE GREAT DEPRESSION*, MOMMA AND THE CHILDREN WERE SOMETIMES ABLE TO *SUPPLEMENT* OUR FAMILY'S MODEST *INCOME* BY TOURING THE COUNTRY *LIP-SYNCING* INSIPID, *WHITE-BREAD* ROCK MUSIC.

PUTTA- PUTTA- PUT!

I KNEW MOMMA WAS COUNTING ON ME AND THAT RESPONSIBILITY BEGAN TO WEIGH HEAVY ON MY SPIRITS.

VRRROOOM!

EL Abe-0

ABE, MY MAN! WHY SO GLUM, BRO?

HEY, *JASON*, *LUKE* AND *TORI-MAE*! MOMMA SENT ME OUT TO FETCH DADDY BACK, AND I CAN'T FIND HIM!

OH, MAN. I *FEEL* YOUR *PAIN*.

LUKE, LIKE, *TOTALLY* KNOWS WHAT PAIN *IS*.

WELL, CHECK IT OUT, *ABE-STER*. WE'RE MEETING *BRENDA* AND *KELLY-SUE* AT THE *TAR PIT*. WANNA HANG WITH US?

GEE, I'D LIKE TO, BUT I CAN'T LET MOMMA DOWN. THAT WOULD BREAK HER HEART.

HEAR YOU, DUDE. *I* FEEL MOMMA'S PAIN, *TOO*!

LUKE IS THE *KING* OF PAIN.

HE IS THE *ANGST-A-GANGSTA!* MY MAIN MAN!

WELL, I GOTTA GET GOING, GUYS. IF I DON'T FIND DADDY SOON THERE'LL BE NO CHRISTMAS ON SIMPSONS MOUNTAIN.

OH, MAN. *NO CHRISTMAS!* I AM IN *SO* MUCH *PAIN!*

FWAP!

OOOPS, SORRY, LUKE! I DIDN'T MEAN TO *UPSET* YOU!

OH, WOW! I'M GONNA GO HOME AND GET DRUNK AND MOPE AROUND AND GET OUT MY GUN AND SHOOT OUT MY STEREO AND THEN BREAK UP WITH MY GIRLFRIEND AND GIVE MY-SELF A NEAR-LETHAL DOSE OF TRIPLE EXPRESSO CAFE' LATTE' AND MOPE AROUND SOME MORE AND THEN DRIVE MY VINTAGE PORSCHE SPEEDSTER OFF OF A CLIFF, MAN!

OOOOH! SOUNDS, LIKE, *UTTERLY TRAGIC,* LUKE. BUT CAN YOU, LIKE DROP US OFF AT THE TAR PIT FIRST?

HEY, NO PROBLEM.

VRRROOOM!

MAN, I KNOW WE'RE IN THE MIDDLE OF *THE GREAT DEPRES-SION,* BUT THAT GUY IS *REALLY* DEPRESSING!

FEELING IN NEED OF A TONIC TO LIFT MY SPIRITS, I STOPPED INTO *IKE GODFREY'S* GENERAL STORE FOR A ROOT BEER...

UH, HELLO, IKE...BOY, YOU SURE HAVE *CHANGED* THE OLD PLACE!

YES. YES. YOU *BET!* I AM THOROUGHLY *MODERNIZED* NOW!

HI DIDDLY HO, BART!

MY NAME IS *ABE-BOY*, SIR.

NOW, NOW, SON. RESPECT YOUR ELDERS.

WOULD YOU CARE TO AVAIL YOURSELF OF OUR NEW SQUISHEE MACHINE?

ALTHOUGH IKE'S REMODELING HAD MADE THE STORE UNRECOGNIZABLE TO ME, AND HIS PRICES WERE ASTRONOMICALLY *HIGH* FOR 1937, I FELT ODDLY AT HOME IN THESE STRANGE SURROUNDINGS.

SLURP!

...ONE MINI-BAG PORK RINDS, $1.29; ONE SIX-PAK DUFF BEER, $3.25; TWO FROZEN CORN-DOG COMBO MEALS, $6.95...

HAVE A NICE DAY!

THAT'S TOTALLY UNBELIEVABLE, GRAMPA. BUT AT *LEAST* IT DOESN'T SOUND LIKE SOMETHING I'VE SEEN ON *TV!*

I DON'T KNOW WHAT WAS IN THAT SQUISHEE, BUT SUDDENLY, ALL THE COLOR DRAINED FROM MY VISION.

THEODORE!

THEODORE...*BEAVER*! YOU ANSWER ME WHEN I CALL YOU, YOUNG MAN!

BUT, I'M *ABE-BOY*, MOMMA!

JEEPERS, BEAV! DON'T TALK BACK TO MOM! YOU WANNA GET *CLOBBERED*?

IT'S ALL RIGHT, WALLY... NOW, BEAVER, YOU RUN ALONG AND FIND YOUR FATHER. I HAVE MILK AND COOKIES WAITING FOR YOU AT HOME, DEAR.

YES, MOMMA.

GOLLY, MOM. HE CAN BE SUCH A LITTLE *CREEP* SOMETIMES!

NOW, WALLY...

HOLD IT, GRAMPA! THESE *RE-RUNS* ARE BAD ENOUGH, BUT DO WE HAVE TO HAVE 'EM IN *BLACK AND WHITE*?!

THE BOY'S GOT A POINT THERE. COULDN'T YOU AT LEAST *COLORIZE* 'EM LIKE THAT *TED FONDA* GUY DOES?

THAT'S *TED TURNER*, DAD!

WILL ALL OF YOU BE QUIET AND LET GRAMPA FINISH HIS STORY?

OKAY, BUT IN COLOR, MAN.

I HAD BEGUN TO DESPAIR OF *EVER* FINDING MY DADDY.

AND THEN I SAW A LONE FIGURE STANDING ON A BRIDGE

PLEASE, *LORD*... I'M SORRY THAT I'D WISHED I'D NEVER BEEN BORN. CLARENCE, *HELP ME!* GET ME *BACK*. I DON'T CARE WHAT HAPPENS TO ME. ONLY GET ME BACK TO MY WIFE AND KIDS! I WANT TO *LIVE* AGAIN!

DADDY? MOMMA SAYS SHE WANTS YOU HOME!

NOW GET OUT OF HERE, BERT, OR I'LL HIT YOU AGAIN! GET OUT.....WHAT? *ABE BOY?* YOU *KNOW* ME, BOY? YOU KNOW WHO I *AM?!*

ZZA-ZZA'S PEDALS! ZZA-ZZA'S...THEY'RE HERE, BERT! WHAT DO YOU KNOW ABOUT THAT! *MERRY CHRISTMAS!*

MOMMA SAYS I'M TO FETCH YOU BACK, DADDY.

WOO-HOO!!!

MERRY CHRISTMAS, SIMPSONS MOUNTAIN! *MERRY CHRISTMAS,* YOU WONDERFUL OL' MOUNTAIN!

OH, GIMME A *BREAK*, GRAMPA! I'VE SEEN *THAT* ON TV A *MILLION TIMES!!*

SHUT UP, BART!!!

OH, MY, *LOOK* AT US! THE PERFECT PICTURE OF A *FAMILY* AT *HOME* ON A WINTER'S EVE!

AT THE RISK OF SOUNDING LIKE A *LUDDITE*... OR WORSE, THE *UNABOMBER*...ONE CAN'T HELP BUT FEEL THAT TECHNOLOGY AND THE ENTERTAINMENT INDUSTRY HAVE SOMEHOW DEADENED OUR *SOULS*, SQUELCHED OUR *HUMANITY*...

YEAH, AND THEY'VE HOT-WIRED GRAMPA'S *MEMORY*, TOO!

IT'S THE WORK OF *SATAN*, I TELL YOU.

WELL, *WE'LL* SHOW 'EM! WE CAN BE A FAMILY *WITHOUT* THIS STUPID BOX! I SAY WE JUST TAKE THAT TV AND *HEAVE* IT RIGHT OUT THE WINDOW!

HEINOUS FUNNIES

DECEMBER, 1933

No. 1

BONGO COMICS GROUP

GROENING
Mouison
Kent

Featuring
ITCHY & SCRATCHY

I AM BLIND

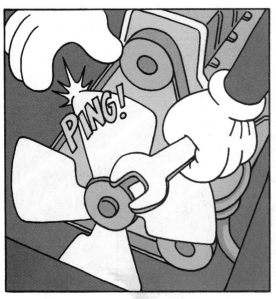

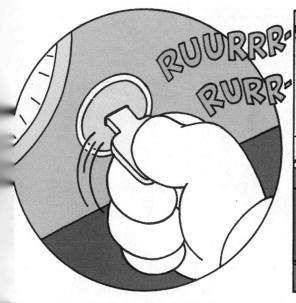

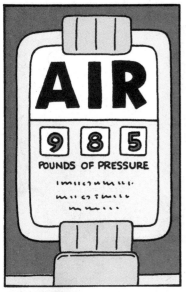

WAITRESSES IN THE SKY

PLEASE! ...I AM AN INNOCENT MAN. I SWEAR BY THE BOUNTIFUL BELLY OF *GANESHA*, I CAN EXPLAIN TO YOU MY ACTIONS.

YOU'RE TOO LATE, MR. NAHASAPEE-WHATEVER.

SCRIPT
LONA WILLIAMS &
JEFF ROSENTHAL

PENCILS
PHIL ORTIZ

INKS
TIM HARKINS

LETTERS
JEANNINE CROWELL

COLOR
NATHAN KANE

AUTOPILOT
MATT GROENING

AAAAAGGGHH!

COMPL

SLAM!

COMPLAINTS

PLEASE! I NEED TO PAY MY FINE TO REMOVE THE DREADED BOOT OF DENVER FROM MY *"KWIK-E-MART-SQUISHEE-KART."*

BAM BAM

I PROMISE TO NEVER AGAIN SELL FROZEN REFRESHMENTS IN THE EMERGENCY LOADING ZONE OF THE HOSPITAL.

DOORS OPEN AT NINE.

CUSTOMER TIME

ACTUAL TIME

MEANWHILE...

PHOTO STATION

OH, I HOPE ONE OF THE TWO PHOTOS IS FLATTERING.

WHIIRRR!

SNIP!

LUCKY YOU. ONE OF THEM IS.

OFFICIAL DMV SPRINGFIELD

SPRINGFIELD OFFICIAL DMV

YOU'LL RECEIVE YOUR NEW LICENSE IN 4-6 MONTHS. NOW AM-SCRAY!

41

A MOMENT LATER...

WELL, LET'S LOOK ON THE BRIGHT SIDE. AT LEAST WE'RE OUT OF WORK TOGETHER.

YOU'RE RIGHT. A SMOKE...TO SISTERHOOD.

JEEZUM CROW, IT'S *EMPTY!* SELMA, HOW MANY CIGARETTES HAVE YOU *HAD* TODAY?

THE USUAL. ONE HUNDRED AND THIRTY-FIVE SINCE BREAKFAST.

THAT'S STRANGE. WE SHOULD HAVE TWO LEFT.

HRUMPH! FIRST WE LOSE OUR *JOBS,* AND NOW WE'RE OUT OF *CIGARETTES.*

WELL, AT LEAST WE'RE *DONE* WITH IT. REMEMBER, GRANDMA ALWAYS SAID, "BAD LUCK COMES IN *TWO'S.*"

THREE'S, PATTY. SHE ONLY SAID *TWO'S* BECAUSE SHE COULDN'T MAKE A *"TH"* SOUND WITHOUT HER *UPPER PLATE* IN.

WE'RE HOME.

THAT SAME EVENING...

♪ MAN ON THE LAM! ♪ HE'S A MAN ON THE LAM. NO LAWMAN CAN... ♪ CATCH THE ♫ MAN ON THE LAM! ♫

SING IT, HOMER!

WE ALL KNOW HE DIDN'T DO IT, SO WHY DO WE WATCH THE SHOW?

WE'RE ALL AWAITING THE FINAL CONFRONTATION BETWEEN HIM AND THE CLUB-FOOTED GUY.

TONIGHT'S EPISODE: SILENCE OF THE MAN ON THE LAM

HOMER, SOMEONE'S AT THE DOOR. WILL YOU PLEASE GO ANSWER IT?

I THOUGHT CASA DE HUEVOS GRANDE WAS YOUR FAVORITE SHOW.

=DING DONG!=

BUT, MARGE, THIS IS MY FAVORITE SHOW!

THAT'S CHANNEL OCHO! THIS IS MY FAVORITE ONE ON CHANNEL SIX.

I THOUGHT THAT WAS MAKE ROOM FOR PRALINES.

THAT'S ON AT NINE O'CLOCK. THIS IS MY FAVORITE CHANNEL SIX SHOW THAT'S ON RIGHT NOW!

YEAH, OKAY. WHATEVER.

MY GOODNESS, ARE YOU ALRIGHT?

SAVE THE SWEET TALK, LITTLE SISTER. WE'RE FINE.

WE JUST NEED A PLACE TO STAY FOR AWHILE, SOME SMOKES, AND A COUCH TO WATCH MACGYVER ON. YOU WON'T EVEN KNOW WE'RE HERE.

THAT NIGHT...

BART, THANKS FOR SHARING YOUR ROOM WITH ME.

ARE YOU *KIDDIN'*? I COULDN'T LET YOU SHARE YOUR ROOM WITH *AUNT SELMA*. THEN I WOULDA' HAD TO SHARE MY ROOM WITH...

≷GULP≶ *AUNT PATTY.*

IN LISA'S ROOM...

HEY, PATTY, TURN OFF THE NIGHT LIGHT. IT'S BEEN A LONG DAY.

AH, TO SLEEP. PERCHANCE TO DREAM OF *CHUCK WOOLERY.*

DO NOT TURN OFF. SAPLINGS WILL DIE.

THE NEXT MORNING...

MOM, *LOOK!* AUNT PATTY AND AUNT SELMA KILLED MY *SAPLINGS!* I WAS SUPPOSED TO SELL THEM AS A SCHOOL PROJECT FOR *EARTH DAY!*

I'M *SORRY,* LISA, I'M SURE THEY DIDN'T *MEAN* IT.

HERE, HONEY, I'LL BUY THEM FROM YOU... I CAN USE THE... SOIL...FOR...SOMETHING.

YOINK!

SORRY, MARGE! YOU *SNOOZE,* YOU *LOSE!*

GLUUMPPH!

AYE, CARUMBA!

IT'S *RUINED!*

BART, I'M VERY SORRY, I'LL GET YOU ANOTHER ONE.

RADIOACTIVE MAN

BUT THIS IS THE CLASSIC, ULTRA-RARE, LIMITED EDITION OF *RADIOACTIVE MAN'S NUCLEAR WINTER WONDERLAND –ABSOLUTE ZERO.*

I HAD TO SEND ALL THE WAY TO *PLATTSBURGH* FOR IT. THERE'S NOT ANOTHER ONE ON THIS PLANET!

MEANWHILE IN PLATTSBURGH...

TOP SECRET DO NOT OPEN!

CAUTION: WRATH OF GOD!

RM-NWW-O QUANTITY:1000 GROSS

RM-NWW-O QUANTITY:1000 GROSS

RM-NWW-O QUANTITY:1000 GROSS

RM NWW-O QUANTITY:1000 GROSS

RM NWW-O QUANTITY:1000

WHOOPS!

LATER...

TIME FOR *YOUR* BREAK-FAST, LITTLE TREES.

BRRR... TOO COLD.

MOMENTS LATER...

WOO HOO! BREAKFAST IS *SERVED!*

THE NEXT DAY...

...SO IN SUMMATION, EITHER *THEY* GO, OR *WE* GO! CAN I GET AN *AMEN*, KIDS??

AMEN, DAD!

PREACH IT, HOMER MAN!

I ADMIT, THEY'RE *OBNOXIOUS* AND *UNGRACIOUS*. BUT THEY'RE MY *SISTERS*. I DON'T KNOW WHAT TO *DO*.

ACK...ACK!

UH, PATTY? SELMA? WE'VE GOT TO TALK.

THAT'S IT! THEY'RE *OUT* OF HERE!

WE SURE *DO*. THAT DOG OF YOURS *REEKS*!

I WAS THINKING WE COULD TALK ABOUT YOU TWO. YOU KNOW, FINDING NEW *JOBS*, LOOKING FOR AN *APARTMENT*...

DO YOU MIND? MACGYVER'S TRAPPED IN AN ABANDONED MINE WITH ONLY HIS WITS, DENTAL FLOSS, AND A TUB OF NON-DAIRY DESSERT TOPPING.

CLICK!

LOOK, I'LL BE BRIEF. YOU TWO NEED TO GET BACK INTO THE WORK FORCE.

A CAREER SHOULD INVOLVE SOMETHING YOU ALREADY ENJOY DOING. SO, FINISH THIS SENTENCE: "I ENJOY..."

SMOKING.

WORKING AT THE *DMV*.

MAYBE WE SHOULD TRY TO LOOK AHEAD. TRY THIS: "NEXT YEAR AT THIS TIME I WOULD LIKE TO BE..."

SMOKING.

WORKING AT THE *DMV*.

OKAY, WELL, SOMETIMES IT'S GOOD JUST TO GET OUT OF THE HOUSE FOR A WHILE.

YOU KNOW, CLEAR YOUR HEAD, GET SOME FRESH AIR...

...AND *GET OUT OF THE HOUSE!* ...FOR AWHILE.

I BELIEVE IT'S A KNOT IN YOUR PERFECTLY DEVELOPED *TRAPEZIUS*, SIR.

HELLO, WHAT'S *THIS*?

C.M.BURNS

WAP! WAR!

NOT *THERE*, YOU NINNY, ON THE *MONITOR*!

WELL, SIR, IT APPEARS THAT TWO MEN DRESSED AS WOMEN ARE PUSHING A LATE MODEL BUICK THROUGH THE MOB OF FLIGHT ATTENDANTS THAT HAVE BEEN PICKETING YOUR AIRLINE.

JUST THINK, SMITHERS. ONE OF THEM COULD DO THE WORK OF *TEN* OF THOSE GLORIFIED, OVERPAID *CAR-HOPS*! MAYBE THEY'RE PART OF A *SUPER RACE* OF FLIGHT ATTENDANTS. I *MUST* HAVE THEM! OFFER THEM JOBS *AT ONCE*!

RIGHT AWAY, SIR.

THAT NIGHT...

ARE YOU *SURE* SMITHERS SAID *FLIGHT ATTENDANTS*? 'CAUSE LENNY SAID THAT THEY WERE LOOKING FOR TWO *CONTAMINATION SHOWER ATTENDANTS*.

LAUGH IT UP, CUE-BALL! LEARNING THE CONTENTS OF THIS MANUAL IS ALL THAT STANDS BETWEEN OUR CAREER IN THE SKY AND LIFE ON EARTH WITH YOU.

AIRLINE SAFETY MANUAL

WOO HOO! LEARN, BABY, LEARN!

OKAY, IT SAYS HERE, "EVEN DURING TURBULENCE, THE PASSENGER IS ENTITLED TO A NICE HOT OR COLD BEVERAGE."

GUT-B GONE

EEEYAAHH! FIRE DOWN BELOW!

AAAAH! IT'S AS IF I'M BURNING IN ETERNAL HELLFIRE!!

SAY, REVEREND, SHOULDN'T YOU WATCH THE H-E-DOUBLE HOCKEY STICKS IN FRONT OF THE KIDDLES?

CLICK!

LATER...

IT SAYS RIGHT HERE THAT "ALL FLIGHT ATTENDANTS MUST KNOW CPR." YOU MAY NEED TO SAVE A LIFE.

OH, YEAH? WELL, I DON'T THINK POPS HERE IS GOING TO MAKE IT!

HEH, HEH! YEAH. I'LL ONLY SAVE THE CUTE ONES.

HELLO? ...I CAN'T FEEL MY SPINE! HELLO??

HOURS PASS...

BYE-BYE.

TOODLEY-OODLES.

LATER.

LADIES, THERE'LL BE NO LOVE LOST IF I DON'T SEE YOU THIS SUNDAY.

SEE YA.

WHICH WAY TO BAGGAGE CLAIM?

WE DID IT! NOW, ALL WE NEED TO DO IS PASS THE WRITTEN TEST TOMORROW.

PIECE O' CAKE!

THE NEXT DAY...

YOU DID VERY WELL ON THE TESTS, *SISTERS BOUVIER*. YOU BOTH HAD ONLY *ONE* INCORRECT ANSWER.

NUMBER 17, REGARDING LOSS OF CABIN PRESSURE. *INFANTS* ARE ENTITLED TO OXYGEN MASKS, *TOO!*

AND WHICH QUESTION WAS THAT?

YOU LIVE, YOU LEARN.

WELL, CLIMB ABOARD AND *GOOD LUCK!*

EVERY NERVE IN MY BODY IS ON *FIRE. FIRE* I TELL YOU, *FIRE!*

I DON'T KNOW HOW MUCH LONGER I CAN *TAKE* THIS, PATTY.

THIS IS TORTURE. SHEER *TORTURE!*

FLIGHT ATTENDANTS PREPARE FOR *TAKE-OFF!*

WHEN IS THE CAPTAIN GONNA TURN OFF THAT SIGN?

NO SMOKING

SOME TIME LATER...

OFF-OFF-OFF-OFF-OFF-OFF-OFF...

NO SMOKING

C'MON, BABY! MAMA NEEDS SOME OF THAT SWEET NIC-O-TINE!

EXCUSE ME, UH, WE'VE BEEN FLYING FOR *TWO HOURS* AND WE HAVEN'T BEEN SERVED A CUP OF COFFEE.

HECK, WE HAVEN'T EVEN BEEN OFFERED *PEANUTS*!

I'M TERRIBLY SORRY FOR THE DELAY. WHO WOULD LIKE SOME FRESH, HONEY-ROASTED PEANUTS?

SHA-DOINK!

HEADS UP, PEOPLE!

OKAY, WHO WANTS A SOFT DRINK WITH THAT?

FINE. IF YOU NEED US WE'LL BE TALKING TO THE CAPTAIN.

COCKPIT

C'MON, SELMA, EITHER THE PILOT LANDS THIS PUPPY OR I PUT HIS NOSE INTO AN UPRIGHT AND LOCKED POSITION.

THAT AFTERNOON...

I'M AFRAID OUR DREAMS OF EVER FINDING THAT PERFECT JOB CRASH LANDED ALONG WITH THE PLANE.

LISTEN, I'M SURE YOU TWO WILL FIND A VOCATION THAT'S NOT ONLY FULFILLING, BUT WHERE THERE ARE NO SMOKING RESTRICTIONS.

RING RING

BOB'S ROADKILL JERKY EMPORIUM, YOU MAKE 'EM FLY, WE'LL MAKE 'EM DRY.

PHOTO STATION

REGISTRATION

I'M SORRY, DAVE, BUT THAT'S NOT POSSIBLE.

DAISY...DAISSSY... GIVE MEEE YOURR ANSSWERRR TRUUUEE...♪

GIVE A HOOT

DON'T DRINK AND DRIVE

WHAT!?! UH, LISTEN, I CAN'T HEAR YOU VERY WELL. IT'S A MADHOUSE HERE! THE PRESIDENTS HAVE GONE HAYWIRE, AND NO ONE IS ANSWERING THE PHONE AT THE AUTOMATION CENTER...

...PLEASE, WE NEED PATTY AND SELMA RIGHT AWAY!

LATER, AT THE DMV...

CUSTOMER TIME

ACTUAL TIME

...YOU SAID TO FOLLOW THE BLUE LINE, SO I FOLLOWED THE BLUE LINE AND THE LADY THERE ASKED ME WHERE MY FORM IS FROM THE RED LINE...

SHA-WAM!

IT'S TOO BAD *GRANDMA* NEVER WORKED AT THE DMV.

WELCOME BACK, SELMA LOVE Patty

WELCOME BACK, PATTY LOVE Selma

...BUT THERE IS NO RED LINE AND I'VE BEEN IN THIS LINE FOR TWO HOURS...

SHE WOULD HAVE *LOVED* IT. IT'S THE *FOUNTAINHEAD* OF BAD LUCK.

JUST ASK ONE OF OUR *CUSTOMERS!*

HEH, HEH!

THE END

...PAY *CLOSE* ATTENTION!

00:06:32

I DON'T KNOW WHAT CAME OVER ME. MAYBE I WAS POSSESSED BY THE SPIRITS OF ALL THE BULLET-RIDDEN, KWIK-E-MART EMPLOYEES WHO WENT BEFORE ME...

LOOK! A DEFENSELESS OLD WOMAN WITH A BROKEN ARM, AND A POCKETBOOK BULGING WITH HUNDRED DOLLAR BILLS!

HUH? *WHERE?*

00:06:40

...OR MAYBE IT WAS TOO MUCH COFFEE.

CHUTNEY

SKLUTCH!

TAKE *THAT* AND TELL ME HOW YOU *LIKE* IT!

YEEAARGH! OH, MAN! THIS FULLY *BITES!*

SLOOSH!

PREPARE TO BE SEVERELY PUMMELED ABOUT THE HEAD AND SHOULDER AREA!!

ANYHOW, AS YOU ARE SEEING, I HAMMERED THE HOLY *SNOT* OUT OF THAT GUY!

THWOK

00:06:52

NEXT, I CALLED 911 AND WAITED FOR THE POLICE TO ARRIVE. BY THE WAY, WHEN YOU HAVE *YOUR* FIRST HOLD-UP, YOU NEED NOT WASTE TIME DIALING ALL THREE NUMBERS. WE HAVE IT ON OUR *SPEED-DIAL* SYSTEM.

00:11:17

MANY HOURS PASSED, AND I BEGAN HAVING TROUBLE STAYING ALERT.

SO TELL ME, MISTER TRAVOLTA, WHAT WAS IT LIKE TO BE DANCING WITH UMA THURMAN IN YOUR FICTITIOUS *PULP* MOVIE?

WHAT? WHERE?

10:46:48

BUT WHY DID YOU NOT TAKE A NAP?

A KWIK-E-CLERK *NEVER* DESERTS HIS POST! ESPECIALLY NOT WHEN THERE IS A DANGEROUS CRIMINAL ON THE PREMISES.

I REMAINED AWAKE BY KEEPING MYSELF BUSY! SEE, HERE I AM CLEANING OUT THE SQUISHEE MACHINE.

11:59:07

HMM...PERHAPS I SHOULD HAVE CLEANED THIS THING OUT AFTER MY *KENTUCKY-FRIED SQUISHEE* EXPERIMENT.

THE LONGER I WAS STAYING AWAKE, THE STRANGER MY ACTIVITIES WERE BECOMING.

A SHRINE TO *GANEESHA* MADE ENTIRELY FROM *BEEF JERKY!*

I WOULD LIKE TO SEE REVEREND LOVEJOY TOP *THIS!*

THE STRANGER MY ACTIONS BECAME, THE LESS I AM REMEMBERING THEM.

LOOK AT ME! I'M CIRCUS BOY! WEEE!

36:15:42

♪ I CAN DO THAT, I CAN DO THAT! THAT I CAN DOOOO! ♪

72:18:23

AT LAST, SALVATION CAME BURSTING THROUGH MY FRONT DOOR.

WHERE *ARE* THEY?

LEMME AT' EM!

96:01:37

THERE HE IS, COLLAPSED IN THAT *PORK-RIND* DISPLAY!

LET'S JUST PRAY TO GOD, HE DIDN'T *CRUSH* 'EM ALL.

BROTHER APU! ARE YOU ALL *RIGHT*?

"AT LAST, MY SHIFT HAD ENDED!"

BZZ...BZZ...THE FLOWERS ARE CALLING *OUT* TO ME...BZZ...THERE IS *MUCH WORK* TO BE DONE...AND I'M *JUST* THE LITTLE HUMMINGBIRD WHO CAN *DO* IT!

QUICKLY! SOMEBODY GET THIS MAN SOME *NECTAR*!

OH, *YEAH!* I CAN *BREATHE* AGAIN!

I THINK MY LUNGS WERE BEGINNING TO LOSE THEIR COATING OF *TAR!*

HEAVEN *FORBID!*

THANK YOU FOR RESCUING ME, BUT *96 HOURS* IS NOT EXACTLY A *SPEEDY* RESPONSE TIME!

OH, DON'T THANK ME.

IT WOULD HAVE TAKEN LONGER IF THE BOUVIER SISTERS HADN'T RUN OUT OF CIGARETTES. IT SEEMS THAT YOUR STORE IS THE ONLY ONE IN TOWN THAT STOCKS THEIR BRAND -- *LADY LARAMIE, FILTER-FREE* WITH 40% MORE *TAR.* THEY TUNNELED THROUGH THAT SNOW IN NO TIME FLAT. NOW, ABOUT THOSE DONUTS...

SO THERE YOU HAVE YOUR LESSON FOR TODAY!

STOP

BUT WHAT HAVE I *LEARNED*, UNCLE APU?

THAT EVEN IF YOU WORK FOR 96 HOURS WITHOUT A SINGLE SALE, YOUR TIME SPENT WORKING IS NEVER A WASTE.

ESPECIALLY IF YOU HAVE A COUSIN WHO WORKS ON THE TV SHOW "AMERICA'S STRANGEST SECURITY CAMERA VIDEOS." TWENTY THOUSAND DOLLAR GRAND PRIZE, COME TO PAPA!

THE END

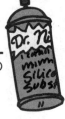

BOY! IS IT BETTER YET?!

A LITTLE TO THE LEFT! TRY BENDING IT *UP* MORE!

BART, STOP TORMENTING YOUR FATHER.

COME ON, MOM. THIS IS THE ONLY WAY I CAN CONTROL THE REMOTE.

I CONTROL THE VERTICAL! *I* CONTROL THE HORIZONTAL!

CLICK!

CLICK!

HELLO, I'M *TROY MCCLURE*. PERHAPS YOU REMEMBER ME FROM *OTHER* TRAVEL SHOWS SUCH AS, *"WHERE THE HECK IS THE PEOPLE'S REPUBLIC OF KAMPUCHEA?"* AND *"BOY, OH CHEBOYGAN!"*...

EYE ON SPRINGFIELD

CLICK!

CLICK!

KENT BROCKMAN HERE, AND IF I DIDN'T KNOW BETTER, I'D SAY THAT THIS *NEXT* SENSATIONAL STORY IS *ABSOLUTELY TRUE*...

HI, EVERYBODY!

TODAY WE'RE GOING TO LEARN ABOUT MY *LATEST* NEW MIRACLE INVENTION: *"H3O"*-- THE *WETTEST* WATER YOU *EVER* TASTED!...

HI, DR. NICK!

WHOA! YOU CAN RENT OUT A WHOLE TV CHANNEL? LIKE IT WAS A *CAR* OR A *GUN* OR SOMETHING?

WELL, MORE LIKE A *CAR*. IT'S PROBABLY A VERY SMALL PUBLIC ACCESS STATION THAT ONLY BROAD-CASTS TO SPRINGFIELD.

THIS CHANNEL FOR RENT

COOL!

HI-DIDDILY-HO, NEIGHBOR. FINALLY TAKING DOWN THAT OLD DINOSAUR, I SEE.

IF YOU *MUST* KNOW, FLANDERS, THIS IS AN *ANTENNA* AND I'M TRYING TO FIX THE *RECEPTION!*

RECEPTION? WELL, NOT THAT I MIND, BUT YOU'VE BEEN SPLICING INTO MY *CABLE LINE* FOR *YEARS* NOW!

YOU DON'T *NEED* AN ANTENNA!

D'OH!!

...THOUGH I *WOULD* LIKE MY WIRE CUTTERS BACK.

THE BOY... MUST PUNISH THE BOY...

YEEARRRRGH!!!

BART! YOU ALMOST *KILLED* ME UP THERE!

UH, OH!

ME, EITHER. I GOT A SWEET TOOTH FOR THIS STUFF.

I CAN'T WAIT TO SEE WHAT THE KRUSTY-DUDE'S GOING TO DO NEXT.

BAM! BAM!

WOW, I CAN'T BELIEVE I'VE FINALLY OUTGROWN THE OLD *"PIE-IN-THE-FACE"* BIT.

HEY, PUT SOMETHING *ELSE* ON! SOMETHING *NEW* THAT'LL HELP US REDISCOVER OUR LOVE AFFAIR WITH *TV!*

DID YOU HEAR THAT, LIS? THAT'S THE SOUND OF A RESTLESS VIEWING PUBLIC. AND DO YOU KNOW WHAT WE SHOULD DO WHEN WE HEAR THAT SOUND?

NO. WE SHOULD FIND OUT ABOUT RENTING THAT PUBLIC ACCESS TV CHANNEL.

IGNORE IT AND KEEP GOING TO THE COMIC STORE?

IT'S NOT THAT SIMPLE, BART. *PUBLIC ACCESS TELEVISION* IS ONE OF THE MOST DEMOCRATIC EXPRESSIONS OF FREE SPEECH AVAILABLE IN THE COUNTRY. ITS DEGENER-ATION AND MISUSE IS *TRULY* A NATIONAL *TRAGEDY*.

COMEDY, TRAGEDY... WHAT'S THE DIFFERENCE, AS LONG AS IT'S ENTERTAINING!

EYE ON NGFIELD

YOU GUYS HAVE TO *DO* SOMETHING! SIMP-TV IS KICKING OUR *BUTTS!* I HAVE A *MORTGAGE,* YOU KNOW!

CALM DOWN, BROCKMAN. WE ALREADY PUT OUR *BEST* MAN ON IT.

YES, IT'S TRUE. *SIMP-TV* --THAT TAWDRY, FLY-BY-NIGHT NEW CHANNEL-- SEEMS TO BE GATHERING FANS AMONG SPRINGFIELD'S MARGINAL AND DISENFRANCHISED. BUT *THIS* REPORTER PREDICTS *SIMP-TV* WILL BE NOTHING MORE THAN A FLASH IN THE PAN.

NO... DON'T TELL ME YOU SENT... *THE MACHINE!*

WE HAD TO. RIGHT ABOUT NOW THE TOUGHEST NEGOTIATOR IN SPRINGFIELD SHOULD BE SITTING DOWN WITH OUR FRIENDS AT SIMP-TV.

IT'S ALMOST TOO CRUEL.

MEANWHILE...

HI, *LIONEL "THE MACHINE" HUTZ,* ATTORNEY AT LAW. SO, IT'S LIKE THIS: THE GUYS AT THE NETWORK WANT YOU TO FOLD UP YOUR OPERATION AND STOP BROADCASTING *SIMP-TV.* WHAT DO YOU SAY?

NO.

LOOK, I HAVE TO GO. WE'VE GOT A WHOLE BLOCK OF PRIMETIME SHOWS TO SCRIPT, REHEARSE AND SHOOT BY...WELL, BY PRIMETIME.

OKAY, THEN. THANKS FOR YOUR TIME.

SOON...

SORRY, FELLAS. THE KID'S *TOUGH.*

THE GUY MAKES 150 MOVIES, AND *NOW* HE DECIDES TO START ACTING.

FELLOW SEMI-CELEBRITIES, THE TIME HAS COME FOR US TO ACT.

WHAT'S -HIS-FACE IS *RIGHT*.

THANK YOU, KRUSTY.

PUT A SOCK IN IT! I'M GETTING KILLED IN THE RATINGS. AND NO *RATINGS* MEAN NO *ADVERTISING*. AND NO *ADVERTISING* MEANS NO *MONEY*. AND NO MONEY MEANS...WELL, THAT ONE'S SELF-EXPLANATORY. WHAT ARE WE GOING TO DO ABOUT *SIMP-TV*?

WHAT IF WE FLOOD THEM OUT WITH MY NEW WONDER PRODUCT, "H3O"-- THE WETTEST WATER YOU *EVER* TASTED?

HOW DID *HE* GET IN HERE? HE ISN'T EVEN A SEMI-CELEBRITY.

WELL, HOW MUCH HAIRPAINT HAVE *YOU* SOLD LATELY, CHUMP? THAT MESHUGUNA IS HOCKING MY NEW LINE OF *ARTIFICIAL HIPS*!

FOCUS, PEOPLE. WE'VE GOT TO COME UP WITH SOMETHING TO STOP THESE GUYS AT *SIMP-TV*. THEY'RE TOTALLY TUNED INTO WHAT THE PUBLIC WANTS. IT'S LIKE THEY'RE SUPER-GENIUSES OR SOMETHING.

82

MEANWHILE, AT THE STUDIO...

WAKE *UP*, BART! WE HAVE AN *EMERGENCY!*

COLONEL KRUSTY 100% CHICK

WHAT? SWING A CRANE IN THERE WITH A DOUBLE-HUNG BOLEX. WE'LL SHOOT IT WITH A SUN GUN AND DUMP DOWN TO HALF-INCH FOR DAILIES.

GET A GRIP, BART. I KNOW YOU'VE BEEN WORKING HARD BUT WE'VE GOT A SITUATION ON OUR HANDS. TAKE A LOOK AT THE *"BAD BOY"* OF *SIMP-TV!*

HEH, HEH...

COLONEL KRUSTY'S 100% LARD-FRIED CHICKEN STRIPS

WHAT ARE YOU TALKING ABOUT? THAT'S CRUEL AND SADISTIC.

HEY, THAT'S NOT BAD.

AND YOUR POINT IS...

BART, THIS WHOLE CHANNEL IS PANDERING TO THE LOWEST COMMON DENOMINATOR IN OUR AUDIENCE. OUTSIDE OF THE AMUSING CONTEXT OF ANIMATED SHOWS AND COMIC BOOKS, THIS KIND OF VIOLENCE IS JUST PLAIN *MEAN*.

BUT IT *SELLS*, SISTER, IT *SELLS!* I'M TAKING THIS CHANNEL TO THE *TOP*, AND I DON'T CARE HOW MANY INNOCENT HEADS GET FLUSHED IN THE PROCESS!

BACK IN THE BOARDROOM...

COME ON, *THINK!* I NEED MY JOB. THE ONLY OTHER THING I'M QUALIFIED FOR IS DITCH-DIGGING, AND THAT'S JUST MURDER ON MY FALLEN ARCHES.

EXCUSE ME, GENTLEMEN, BUT PERHAPS I CAN BE OF SOME ASSISTANCE.

GASP!

AAAAH!

YOU!

I MIGHT HAVE A WAY TO STOP THESE MEDDLESOME MAYHEM-MAKERS RIGHT IN THEIR TRACKS.

BURNS! WHY WOULD *YOU* WANT TO HELP *US?*

YEAH, WOULDN'T IT BE MORE YOUR STYLE TO GO OUT AND *BUY* SIMP-TV AND THEN TRY TO *BURY* US?

THAT'S A HORRIBLE, CYNICAL THING TO SAY, BROCKMAN. BESIDES, THE FCC PROHIBITS ME FROM PURCHASING ANOTHER BROADCAST NETWORK.

THAT REMINDS ME, SMITHERS. WE NEED TO FIND SOME RUBE TO BUY *ZOO-SPAN.* APPARENTLY NO ONE WANTS TO WATCH CAGED ANIMALS SCRATCH THEMSELVES 24 HOURS A DAY.

MONKEYS ARE FUNNY...

OKAY, WHAT'S THE PLAN, BURNS?

I'LL REVEAL MY SCHEME ONLY IF YOU ALL PROMISE TO HAVE ME ON EACH OF YOUR PROGRAMS AS A FEATURED GUEST STAR. PERHAPS YOU DIDN'T KNOW THIS, BUT I CAN TAP DANCE A PRETTY MEAN BUCK AND WING.

I CAN'T WAIT. YOU'RE ON.

DEAL.

OH, WHAT A TANGLED WEB WE WEAVE...*

OKEY DOKEY!

EXCELLENT. YOU SEE, GENTLEMEN, ALL IT TAKES IS A SIMPLE PHONE CALL...

*SIR WALTER SCOTT, THE LAY OF THE LOST MINSTREL, CANTO IV, STANZA 17

AT THE HOME OF REV. AND MRS. LOVEJOY...

STAY TUNED FOR *"A VERY BRADY BAPTISM"*...

RING-A-RING!

HELLO? YES, INDEED. WHAT? THIS CAN'T BE *TRUE!* IT'S A *SCANDAL!*

SWEET BLISTERING ISAIAH, LOVEY! TURN TO *CHANNEL* 10!

SLAM!

CLICK!

SO THEN *I* SAID, "IN ALABAMA, THE *TUSCALOOSA!* GET IT? THE TUSC-A-*LOOS*-A!"

THIS IS AN ABOMINATION! NOT ONLY IS HE MALIGNING THE GREAT BIBLE–BELT STATE OF ALABAMA, BUT THAT'S THE WORST *ALAN ALDA* IMPRESSION I'VE EVER *SEEN!* THANK YOU, ANONYMOUS STRANGER. I'LL TAKE IT FROM HERE.

SIMPTU

SMITHERS! GET ME MY *TAP SHOES.*

THUNK!

LATER THAT WEEK...

WELL, SO MUCH FOR BURNS' SURE-FIRE SCHEME.

LOOK AT THE BRIGHT SIDE, FELLAS. AT LEAST WE DON'T HAVE TO PUT HIM ON OUR SHOWS.

TRUE. BUT OUR CAREERS MAY WELL BE OVER.

IT IS A TALE TOLD BY AN IDIOT, FULL OF SOUND AND FURY, SIGNIFYING NOTHING.*

*WILLIAM SHAKESPEARE, MACBETH, ACT 5, SCENE 5

HA, HA!

WHY IS THAT SO FUNNY?

BACK AT THE STUDIO...

I AM TOTALLY EXHAUSTED. YOU KNOW WHAT'S THE WORST PART ABOUT *MAKING* TV? I DON'T HAVE ANY TIME TO *WATCH* IT.

YEAH. I HAVEN'T SEEN ANYTHING SINCE *SWEEPS*. LET'S SEE WHAT'S ON.

CLICK!

ONE WEEK LATER...

WHAT'S *WRONG* WITH YOU, *TV*? WHY DON'T YOU HAVE ANYTHING *DECENT* ON?

CLICK!

SIMP-TV CLOSES DOORS FOR UNKNOWN REASONS ALL SHOWS CANCELLED

WIGGUM JUMPS SHIP, BUZZES OVER TO BEE-MAN

MMM, MMM, PASTE TASTES *GOOD!*

CLICK!

AY AY AY, NO ES *BUENO!*

HA, HA! I'M NO COLLEGE GRAD, BUT I KNOW FUNNY. AND *THAT'S* FUNNY!

I DON'T KNOW. I WOULD HAVE LIT RALPH FROM *BELOW* AND SHOT THE WHOLE KITCHEN WITH A *WIDE-ANGLE.*

HA, HA. NO ES BUENO... HOO, HA, HA!

LET IT GO, BART. JUST LET IT GO.

THE END

90

SCRIPT-PENCILS
SCOTT SHAW

TRANSLATION
SERGIO ARAGONES

INKS
BILL MORRISON

LETTERS
JEANNINE CROWELL

COLOR
NATHAN KANE

1. ISAAC WATTS, *AGAINST IDLENESS AND MISCHIEF*
2. WILLIAM SHAKESPEARE, *KING LEAR*, V.II
3. W.S., *CYMBELINE*, III.II
4. W.S., *AS YOU LIKE IT*, I.III

HEY, FRIEND! THE NAME'S *OTTO*. I DRIVE A BUS. ON THE ROAD OF *BROKEN DREAMS* AND *SPRAINED ASPIRATIONS*, HARD HEARTS USUALLY *DON'T* BOUNCE BACK. BUT ONCE IN A WHILE, THE *HIGHLY UNLIKELY* HAPPENS: THE KIDS SAVE THE FARM OR THE PALOOKA GOES THE DISTANCE DESPITE ALL THE ODDS. I SAW IT HAPPEN ONCE AT MOE'S. IT WAS THE BEST STOP ON THE ROUTE--WHERE EVERY JALOPY-JOCKEY PULLED OVER FOR THE STRONGEST JOE THIS SIDE OF DIMAGGIO AND FOOD LIKE GRANNY USED TO MAKE--IF YOU GREW UP IN A *BUS STATION*. A SHORT ORDER GREASE DEALER WITH A SHORTER TEMPER OWNED THE JOINT...

A PACK A DAY for a healthier tomorrow

Buy LARAMIE: an Rx for ...FLAVOR!

Real Pie

HEY, OTTO, FEEL FREE TO NURSE THAT *ONE* LOUSY SODA A FEW MORE *HOURS*.

...HE HAD A HEART LIKE A WEEK OLD CHEESE DANISH; *RANCID AND HARD!* BUT THAT DANISH WAS ABOUT TO...OH, HEY, MAN, I DON'T WANNA GIVE AWAY THE ENDING. IT ALL WENT DOWN IN A STORY I CALL...

THE DAME AND THE CLOWN

SCRIPT:	PENCILS:	INKS:	LETTERS:	COLORS:	SODA JERK:
Clay Griffith	Sharon Bridgeman	David Mowry	Jeannine Crowell	Nathan Kane	Matt Groening

SO LONG, MOE. GOTTA GO REV UP THE REDEYE TO SPRINGFIELD. STAY FROSTY, MAN.

YEAH, THANKS FOR *WEARIN' OUT* MY STOOL!

OH, EXCUSE ME. I DIDN'T SEE YOU THROUGH THE TEARS.

WHOA, DOLL! YOU MUST HAVE HAD THE *SCRAPPLE*...

COFFEE, PLEASE.

:SIGH: OKAY.

ALL RIGHT, BUT I DON'T WANT TO HEAR YOUR *PROBLEMS*.

Real Pie

IT'S HOUSE RULES. *NO PROBLEMS*.

I'M GOOD AT SUPPRESSING MY FEELINGS.

OH, MY. WHAT A *LOVELY* PIE CAROUSEL.

REALLY?

YOU REALLY LIKE IT? IT WAS MY *SAINTED MOTHER'S*!

OH, YEAH! SHE LEFT IT TO ME ON HER DEATHBED. "MOE," SHE SAID, "YOU'RE THE ONLY ONE WHO *REALLY* LOVED ME. TAKE THE *PIE THINGY*..."

OH, MA!

THERE, THERE...

ER...UH...*HEY!* DON'T *SOFT-SOAP* ME BY FLATTERING MA'S PIE CAROUSEL.

SORRY. NO OFFENSE.

NOW BOARDING THE 11:15 TO SPRINGFIELD!

OH, HOMER. IF ONLY I COULD AFFORD A TICKET BACK HOME TO YOU.

HEY! I HEARD *THAT!*

I *WARNED* YOU! KEEP IT TO YOURSELF!

Ahoy from your Homey

HEY, *HEY!* UH... I MEAN... *THERE* YOU ARE!

OH, *DEAR!* HE *FOUND* ME!

BABY, I BURNED A LOT OF *BIG SHOE LEATHER* LOOKING FOR *YOU!*

OPE

FIN.

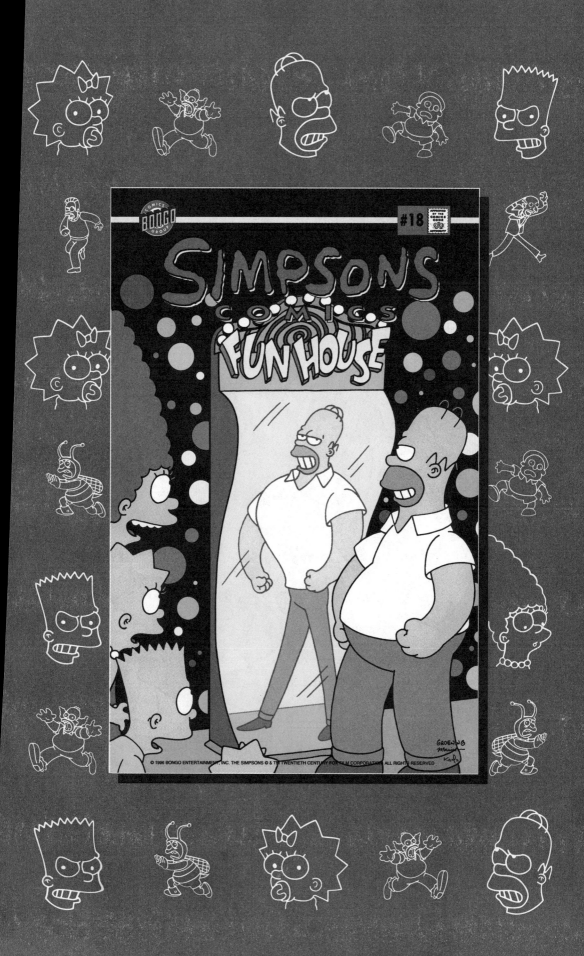

GET FATTY

C.I.A. HEADQUARTERS
WASHINGTON, D.C.

LETS PLAY A GAME--
I SPY SOMETHING *WEAK*
AND *PATHETIC!*

NOT AGAIN!

≥CHOKE!≥

SCRIPT	PENCILS -- ART SUPERVISION	INKS
GARY GLASBERG	STEPHANIE GLADDEN	TIM HARKINS
LETTERS	COLORS	MR. OLYMPIA
JEANNINE CROWELL	NATHAN KANE	MATT GROENING

KNOCK OFF THE *THEATRICS*, WOLFCASTLE! WHO DO YOU THINK *CLEANS UP* THIS MESS EVERY TIME YOU SHOW UP?

BEATS ME. TEAMSTAHS?

GO AHEAD IN. HE'S *EXPECTING* YOU. BUT REMEMBER, DON'T SAY ANYTHING ABOUT HIS WEIGHT OR THAT INCIDENT WHEN YOU...

• PRESIDENT •

==SLAM!==

HIYA, *TUBBY!* I HAVEN'T SEEN YOU SINCE *OCTOBAHFEST* AT *CAMP DAVID* WHEN *TOMMY TUNE* AND *I* STOPPED YOU FROM DOING *"SINGING IN DA RAIN"* UNDAH DA BIDET!

SIT DOWN, RAINIER. WE HAVE A CRISIS ON OUR HANDS THAT POSES A *SEVERE THREAT* TO NATIONAL SECURITY.

CHOMP! CHOMP!

DA ONLY TING I SEE ON YOUR HANDS, MR. PRESIDENT, IS *SPECIAL SAUCE.*

USING OUR OWN SURVEILLANCE SATELLITES, WE'VE DETECTED SOMETHING *TRULY HORRIFYING* RIGHT HERE IN OUR OWN BACKYARD!

I KNOW, I KNOW. DAT *MOESHA* SHOW IS TOTALLY OUT OF CONTROL.

HOUSE O' DONUTS

GR—
RE-O

PORK SQUEEZINS

DEEP IN THE HEART OF THIS GREAT LAND, LIES A COMMUNITY WHOSE CITIZENS APPEAR TO PRIDE THEMSELVES ON *OVER-INDULGENCE*...

EMBARRASSING THEMSELVES...

AND HAVING THE *WORST* CHOLESTEROL COUNT IN MODERN HISTORY!

LARD
A TUB A DAY IS ALL WE ASK

RAINIER, AS FITNESS AMBASSADOR, I NEED YOU TO TAKE ON SPRINGFIELD'S WORST OFFENDERS AND WHIP THEM INTO SHAPE. OUR NATION NEEDS YOUR HELP!

NORMALLY, I'D HAVE TO PASS, BUT DEY JUST PUSHED BACK THE SHOOTING SCHEDULE FOR MY *NEW* MUSICAL, "MCBAINIE GET YOUR GUN."

HAVE MY SECRETARY HOLD MY CALLS--IT'S TIME TO KICK SOME *CELLULITE*.

LATER...

LYDIA, DID I...AH... GET ANY CALLS?

JUST THE *PRESIDENT*, SIR.

TELL HIM TO MAKE THE CHECK OUT TO "*CASH!*"

I DON'T THINK THAT'S WHAT HE'S CALLING ABOUT, SIR. WE SEEM TO BE UNDER SOME KIND OF *ASSAULT*.

THE CITY'S PANICKING, MR. MAYOR.

THERE'S A *RIOT* AT THE BOWLING ALLEY-- THE SNACK BAR'S SERVING *STEAMED VEGETABLES!*

I KNEW THERE'D BE A *VEGAN REVOLT* SOMEDAY! BLASTED HEALTH FREAKS! I WANT THE...ERR.. NATIONAL GUARD TO SURROUND EVERY HOT DOG CART AND CHEESE STEAK JOINT IN THE CITY. CHUNKY PEOPLE MEAN CHUNKY DONATIONS!

IF THAT DOESN'T WORK, CALL....

SMASH!

KRACK!

WOLFCASTLE!!

BY *ORDER* OF DA *PRESIDENT*, QUIMBY, LET'S TALK *LOWFAT TURKEY!*

COMPANY-SUPPLIED CARBOS WITHIN REACH... *MUST HANG ON...*

CRUUUD!!!

Crudités Here to Stay!

LATER...

HAND OVER THE REMOTE, LISA. THERE'S A GREAT *FOREIGN FILM* ON CHANNEL FIVE!

SINCE WHEN ARE *YOU* INTERESTED IN FOREIGN FILMS?

SNATCH!

SINCE THE CRITICALLY-ACCLAIMED RELEASE OF *"LIKE WATER FOR BRATWURST."*

AND NOW, A *SPECIAL REPORT* FROM CITY HALL.

GOOD PEOPLE OF SPRINGFIELD, LAY DOWN YOUR *CORN DOGS* AND *COCONUT SNOWBALLS* AND... ER...LISTEN TO ME.

THAT MEANS *YOU*, JUMBO!

D'OH!

UNCLE SAM NEEDS YOU TO FACE YOUR GREATEST ADVERSARY...THE MIGHTY *MID-SECTION*...THE *CELLULITE ASSASSINS*...*THE BIG BUTT BRIGADE!*

THE PEOPLE ON THIS LIST HAVE CAUSED SPRINGFIELD TO BE VOTED THE MOST *UNHEALTHY* CITY IN *HISTORY*. THEREFORE, THE WORST WEIGHT OFFENDERS HAVE *TWO WEEKS* TO LOSE *TEN POUNDS*. IF YOU'RE SUCCESSFUL, THE PRESIDENT WILL REWARD OUR FAIR CITY WITH A *WATER PARK* FOR YOUR... AH...SUMMER ENJOYMENT. IF YOU FAIL...

CHIEF CLANCY WIGGUM
BARNEY GUMBLE
DR. JULIUS HIBBERT
RALPH WIGGUM
NELSON MUNTZ
ABE SIMPSON
HOMER SIMPSON
APU NAHASPEEMAPETILON
KRUSTY THE CLOWN
MARTIN PRINCE
KENT BROCKMAN

YOU'LL SPEND *ONE YEAR* AT *SHELBYVILLE MAXIMUM SECURITY FAT FARM!*

OH, DEAR! THE SITE OF THE *GREAT CRULLER UPRISING OF 1982!* TO THIS DAY, THEY HAVEN'T BEEN ABLE TO REMOVE THE *GREASE STAINS* FROM THE WALLS!

LAY OFF THE SNICKERDOODLES, HOMER, OR YOU'LL BECOME KNOWN AS "THE FAT MAN OF ALCATRAZ!"

WHY YOU LITTLE...!

FATTICA! FATTICA!

DAY ONE...

THEY'RE NOT HEAVY, THEY'RE MY BRETHREN

WELL, CLIP MY COOKIE DUSTER! *LOOK* AT THIS TURNOUT!

I HAVEN'T SEEN DIS MANY LARDBOTTOMS SINCE I JUDGED THE "BOSS HOGG LOOK-ALIKE CONTEST" IN '81!

I'M OK YOU'RE NOT

I WANT TO THANK ALL YOU FOLKS FOR COMING TO TODAY'S BIG CHURCHGOERS AEROBICS CLASS.

THERE'S NOTHING LIKE A WORKOUT TO THE BEST OF BURL IVES!

OH, JIMMY CRACK CORN, AND I DON'T CARE... ♪

DAY TWO...

ALL RIGHT, MEN. ARE YOU READY?

ACH! WHATTA YE *WAITIN'* FER? DYOO IT! *NAB* THE *PORKER!*

El Barto

STOP HIM! THE LAD'S FLUSHING THE EVIDENCE!

KVUMP!

DAY THREE...

:SIGH:

...DO YOU FEEL ANYTHING YET, SELMA?

I'M *EXHAUSTED.* HOW ABOUT A CIGA-RETTE BREAK?

NO TIME FOR *BUTTS,* LADIES! YOU TWO GOT MORE *BUTT* DAN YOU NEED *ALREADY!*

DAY FOUR...

TEN MORE MILES, WIGGUM. YOU CAN DO IT!

KEEP YOUR EYES ON THE PRIZE!

0.2 MPH

I LOVE THE SMELL OF SWEAT AND ANCHOVIES IN THE MORNING! SMELLS LIKE... *SWEATY ANCHOVIES!*

DAY FIVE...

YO, LISA! WHAT'S THE BIG HOLD UP?!

HAVEN'T YOU HEARD, OTTO? KRUSTY'S SELLING "SOY GOY: THE KOSHER VEGETARIAN BURGER."

WHO WANTS AVOCADO AND EXTRA SPROUTS? THERE'S PLENTY FOR ALL YOU SALAD-HAPPY SAPS!

CHING!

ELSEWHERE...

HEY, APU. GIVE ME A COTTON CANDY FLAVORED SQUISHEE AND A "HEART STOPPER" 14-LAYER MICROWAVE BURRITO.

NO CAN DO, BART. WE ARE ONLY SELLING WHEATGRASS SQUISHEES NOW. HOW WOULD YOU LIKE ONE WITH EXTRA BEE POLLEN?

THWACK!

THE DAY I PRAYED WOULD NEVER COME IS UPON US...

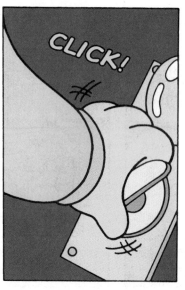

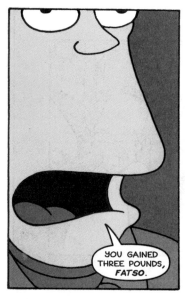

YOU GAINED THREE POUNDS, *FATSO.*

HISS!

BOO!

FATSO!

BOO!

HISS!

YA LOSER!

BOO!

GET OUT OF TOWN, SIMPSON! YOU'RE *RUINING* IT FOR ALL OF US!

IF YOU EVER COME NEAR MY *BEER NUTS* AGAIN, HOMER, I'LL *KILL* YA!

THERE, THERE NEIGHBOR. I KNOW JUST HOW YOU FEEL.

I HAVE THE DARNDEST TIME CONTROLLING *MY* HABIT OF COMFORTING PEOPLE AT *INAPPROPRIATE TIMES.*

ACH, YE SHOULD'VE TRIED MY *HAGGIS AND GRAPEFRUIT DIET!*

WHAT A LET DOWN, SIMPSON! IF YOU WERE ONE OF MY STUDENTS, I'D *EXPEL* YOU!

YOU'RE A *DISGRACE*, HOMER. EVEN I LOST WEIGHT AND ALL I DID WAS *BATHE*!

SO MUCH FOR A WATER PARK FILLED WITH KILLER BABES! MISTER S., YOU HOSED US ALL *BIG TIME*!

LATER...

LOOK AT YOURSELF. YOU'RE AN *EMBARRASS-MENT*. YOU'VE *HUMILIATED* YOUR WHOLE FAMILY.

PORK RINDS

YOU LET YOURSELF GO, SIMPSON. YOU GAVE IN TO THE HYPNOTIC CALL OF CEREAL FUN PACKS AND MICROWAVEABLE SANDWICH POCKETS. YOU HAVE NO CHOICE BUT TO PACK YOUR BAGS AND LEAVE UNTIL ALL THIS BLOWS OVER!

HOMEY?

MY FAMILY! I KNEW I COULD COUNT ON YOU! YOU'VE COME TO STAND BEHIND YOUR CHUBBY OLD MAN!

NOT SO FAST, MAN. AS *EASY* AS IT IS TO STAND "BEHIND" YOU, WE'VE GOT SOMETHING TO SAY!

THE SIMPSON FAMILY IS A *TEAM,* DAD, BUT YOU LET US DOWN!

SHAPE UP, HOMER. IF YOU DON'T WANT TO DO IT FOR THE TOWN, DO IT FOR *US* INSTEAD!

BUT LOOK AT ME! HOW CAN I LOSE *THIRTEEN POUNDS* IN ONE WEEK?! I'LL HAVE TO RESORT TO SOME KIND OF *APPETITE SUPPRESSANT!*

NO PROBLEMO, DUDE!

BEHOLD! A PHOTO OF AUNT PATTY AND AUNT SELMA WHEN THEY WON THAT *LADY LARAMIE HARD BODIES BIKINI CONTEST!*

YEEEAAA!

GOOD WORK, BOY!

I, HOMER SIMPSON, WILL *LOSE WEIGHT.*

I WILL MAKE MY FRIENDS AND FAMILY PROUD!!

DAY THIRTEEN...

YOU AH *HOMAH*!!!!

IN YOUR *FACE*, TASTY BREAKFAST TREAT!

DAY FOURTEEN...

WELL...AH...SIMPSON, *EVERYONE'S* WEIGHED IN. IT'S ALL UP TO *YOU*.

GOOD LUCK, *HOMAH*.

IF IT DOESN'T WORK OUT, YOU CAN COME WORK FOR ME IN *HOLLYWOOD*. I NEED SOMEONE TO *CLEAN* DA *STALLS* OF MY *LLAMA* RANCH!

MAYBE I SHOULDN'T HAVE EATEN THAT *GREEN BEAN* FOR DINNER LAST NIGHT!

DON'T WORRY, HOMEY. REMEMBER, WE *BELIEVE* IN YOU!

¡GULP!¿

240 250 260

¡GASP!¿

12 POUNDS, 15 OUNCES...YOU *DIDN'T* MAKE IT, SIMPSON!

EDITOR'S NOTE: NOT A RECOMMENDED METHOD OF WEIGHT LOSS!

BART'S PAL,

Milhouse

#1

BONGO

2ND BANANA

MILHOUSE
IN
"THE QUEST FOR YAZ"

OKAY, I'VE *FINALLY* SAVED UP ENOUGH FOR THE 1973 CARL YASTZREMSKI "MUTTON CHOP YAZ" BASEBALL CARD. HAND OVER THOSE SWEET SIDEBURNS!

NOT LIKELY. YOU SEE, THE $30 IN YOUR *LESS-THAN-TIDY* HANDS REFLECTS ONLY *HALF* THE CURRENT VALUE OF YE OLDE MUTTON CHOP YAZ.

DO I LOOK LIKE *I* CONTROL THE BASEBALL CARD MARKET? I THINK NOT.

WUH? BUT YOU SAID IT WAS $30.

THE INVISIBLE HAND OF THE MARKETPLACE WORKS IN UNPREDICTABLE, BUT PROFITABLE WAYS. AND SAID INVISIBLE HAND HAS DEEMED THAT *YOU* HAVE TO COUGH UP 60 *BONES* BEFORE YOU SEE SIDEBURN ONE.

YOU BREAK THE FOIL STAMP YOU'VE BOUGHT IT!!

YOU MUST BE THIS TALL "N ANDROIDS OMICS

BANNED FOR LIFE

$100

I DON'T KNOW ABOUT ANY "INVISIBLE HANDS," BUT THAT SOUNDS LIKE *PRICE GOUGING* TO ME.

THAT'S IT! BY YOUR USE OF THE "G" WORD YOU HAVE BESMIRCHED THE GOOD NAME OF THE ANDROID'S DUNGEON. I HATE TO DO THIS, BUT RULES ARE RULES...

SHWOK!

VREEEEEEE!

HEY!

BANNED FOR LIFE

CONGRATULATIONS. YOU ARE NOW *BANNED FOR LIFE* FROM THIS ESTABLISHMENT.

AND THIS IS THE *MLB* "BANNED FOR LIFE." NOT THE SISSY *NBA* OR *NFL* KIND, WHERE A QUICK JAUNT TO THE TREMBLING HILLS CLINIC WILL GET YOU BACK IN. NOW, *VACATE* THE PREMISES BEFORE I RUN YOU THROUGH WITH MY OFFICIALLY LICENSED D&D *DIE-CAST BROADSWORD*.

AWW, *PLEASE* GIMME A SECOND CHANCE!

CARD

WHO NEEDS HIS CRUMMY OLD STORE ANYWAY? SOMEDAY, THE KIDS OF SPRINGFIELD WILL DISCOVER *MAIL-ORDER*, AND THEN *HE'LL* BE SORRY.

OPEN

I HEARD THAT!

WOW! MY VERY OWN *YAZ CARD!* WAIT 'TIL BART SEES *THIS!* NEXT TO THAT KID WHO GOT THE WILLIE DIPKIN "FISHFACE" CARD FOR CHRISTMAS, I'M THE *HAPPIEST* GUY IN SPRINGFIELD.

ARE YOU *REALLY?*

WHO *SAID* THAT?

I DID. I'M *HERE*--IN YOUR *BACK POCKET.*

MUTTON CHOP YAZ!? WOW, A BASEBALL CARD THAT CAN *TALK!*

I CAN'T *REALLY* TALK. THIS IS JUST A DAYDREAM FORCED UPON YOU BY YOUR *GUILT-RIDDEN* CONSCIENCE.

BUT I ONLY STOLE YOU 'CAUSE I'M YOUR BIGGEST FAN. I'VE BEEN WAITING MY *WHOLE LIFE* FOR YOU.

CARL YASTRZEMSKI
BOSTON RED SOX

NO *TRUE* FAN OF MINE WOULD STEAL TO GET MY BASEBALL CARD.

THE PROPER SOURCE FOR BASEBALL CARDS IS ANY OF THE SEEMINGLY *ENDLESS* STRING OF BASEBALL CARD SHOPS. THEIR UNABASHED PROFITEERING HAS BECOME AS AMERICAN AS APPLE PIE AND FREE AGENCY.

I S'POSE YOU'RE RIGHT. I KNEW SOMETHING WAS BOTHERING ME, BUT I JUST THOUGHT I DRANK MY *TANDOORI CHICKEN FLAVORED SQUISHEE* TOO FAST. I GUESS IT MUST BE THE GUILT.

THERE'S ONLY ONE WAY TO UN-BURDEN YOUR CONSCIENCE. YOU MUST *RETURN ME* TO MY RIGHTFUL PLACE IN THE SPOKES OF RALPH'S BICYCLE.

LATER, AT THE WIGGUM HOUSE...

IF CHIEF WIGGUM AND RALPH KEEP PLAYING FETCH, THEY WON'T SEE ME SNEAKING IN THE BACK.

CRASH!

OUCH!

I NEED TO DISTRACT RALPH.

HEY PONCH, I THINK I SAW A *SPEEDER* UNDER THE BED.

WOW, NOW WE CAN GO FIND R2-D2!

NOW'S MY CHANCE TO PUT YOU BACK IN YOUR PLACE, YAZ. CAN'T... REACH...THE...BIKE...

OH, NO, I'M TRAPPED IN THE CAVE...*YEEEOW!*

WHAT'S GOING ON HERE, BOY? YOU KNOW HOW LOUD NOISES MAKE ME NERVOUS.

I THINK RALPH IS STUCK UNDER THE BED.

THERE YOU GO, SON. I'M RELEASING YOU ON YOUR OWN *RECOGNIZANCE*... HEH, HEH, I JUST *LOVE* SAYING THAT...

AT *LAST!* YAZ IS BACK WHERE HE BELONGS. NOW I CAN *SCRAM*.

EVIDENCE

MILHOUSE, COME BACK! WE HAVEN'T PLAYED MY *CUTTHROAT ISLAND* VIDEO GAME YET!

UHHH... I THINK I HEAR MY MOM CALLING ME!

I DON'T HEAR ANYTHING.

WELL...SHE HAS A REALLY HIGH VOICE. ONLY *I* CAN HEAR IT.

CRASH!

YOU ALMOST WRECKED THESE COUNTERFEIT BASEBALL CARDS WE SEIZED.

FAKE⁉ YOU MEAN NONE OF THEM ARE *REAL?*

BETWEEN YOU AND ME, THESE, BASEBALL CARDS ARE ABOUT AS REAL AS MY *DIPLOMA* FROM THE *POLICE ACADEMY.* I USE 'EM AS BEER COASTERS.

AND SO, WITH HIS POCKETS BEREFT OF BOOSTED BASEBALL CARDS (BRUMMAGEM OR BONA FIDE), MILHOUSE LEFT THE WIGGUM HOME KNOWING HE DID THE RIGHT THING.

AND ON THAT DAY HE SWORE A SOLEMN OATH TO PAY ANY *PRICE,* BEAR ANY *BURDEN,* MEET ANY *HARDSHIP,* SUPPORT ANY *FRIEND,* AND OPPOSE ANY FOE TO ASSURE THE SUCCESS AND SURVIVAL OF...

THE QUEST FOR YAZ

CARL YASTRZEMSKI 1st BASE
BOSTON RED SOX

THE END

ADAM FEIN
SCRIPT

CHRIS ROMAN
PENCILS

TIM BAVINGTON
INKS

JEANNINE CROWELL
LETTERS

PETER ALEXANDER
COLORS

MATT GROENING
THE GREEN MONSTER